TEACH ME YOUR WAY

A Year in the Catholic Church

William E. Bullis

Biblical references are drawn from the New American Bible Revised Edition.

Teach Me Your Way / William Emory Bullis

Hardcover ISBN: 979-8-9986328-3-9
Paperback ISBN: 979-8-9986328-2-2

FOR MY LOVE, LESLIE.

CONTENTS

INTRODUCTION

I asked myself while sitting in my car one Sunday, "*I wonder what God wanted me to take away from Mass today? What shall I do as a result?*"

I happened to have a pen and paper, so I wrote it down—the 'takeaway,' that is.

I tried to make it as succinct as I possibly could, aiming for the "one thing" I could learn / understand / imbue / act upon i.e. *takeaway* from all I heard at that particular mass. I kept at it for a few weeks and then figured *why not do this for the whole year?*

What follows is a year of parking lot reflections in the front seat of my car immediately after Mass at Saint Ferdinand's Catholic Church in Pennsylvania.

I estimate that I stuck with my initial "parking lot *takeaway*" more than ninety-five percent of the time. It seemed prudent not to change what my gut told me in the moment. It still does.

However, there were a few weeks when the takeaway was self-evident in scripture and a particular verse seemed to be the best way to articulate it. This was mostly true during weeks where the Gospel told of a miracle or a great event in Jesus' life. You'll see these clearly in what follows.

Towards the end of the year, I looked at my notebook and wondered, "*What am I supposed to do with all of this?*" After weeks of pondering, I felt the answer.

You need to write a prayer.

Interestingly, I'd never *written* a prayer before, but I figured if I could take it all in – the scripture, the homilies, the prayer and reflection - during this year in the Church, and pray accordingly, then perhaps I might come closer to building up my character and increase my chances of meeting Jesus' expectations for me.

Worried, self-centered, anxious, prideful...

I knew those were not what Jesus wanted for me. Then I remembered Psalm 25.

"Make me know your ways Lord;
Teach me your paths." Psalm 25:4

Teach me? I can learn!
Path? I need a map!
Your way, not my way? I'm in!

So I prayed, "Dear Jesus, please teach me your way, not my way. Your way, not my way. Your way, not my way. Your way, not my way..."

Eventually, this developed into the prayer at the end of this book. I hope you find it beneficial, but more importantly I hope you develop your own prayer(s) and pray them for all you're worth, for it seems to me this is how we find our Lord's way and walk in it.

May God bless you!

William E. Bullis, Pennsylvania, U.S.A

BACKGROUND

Scripture, tradition, priestly homilies and prayer provide a limitless fount of inspiration and understanding.

Truth is, it is a fool's errand to try to come up with one, singular takeaway from Sunday mass. Despite this, what follows is the result of this fool's attempt during 2014.

Therefore, let me explain what this year looked like from the liturgical (i.e. public, official worship) perspective of the Catholic Church.

The liturgical year in the Church is centered around significant moments in the life of Jesus, including the annunciation and anticipation of his birth (Advent), his birth, epiphany and baptism (Christmas), his journey to the crucifixion (Lent), his passion and death (Triduum) and his resurrection (Easter). Between the end of Christmas, which is marked by the baptism of Jesus, and the beginning of Lent we enter into Ordinary Time. This (Ordinary Time) is interrupted by Easter and begins again after Pentecost and ends again when Advent begins. Special feasts during Ordinary Time are known by their title, for example the Feast of Christ the King.

The Roman Rite (i.e. the liturgical traditions of the Latin (Western) Church) celebrates Sunday liturgies following a three-year cycle that is identified as Year A, B and C. These then designate which Synoptic Gospel will be used during that liturgical year. Year A draws from the Gospel of Matthew, Year B the Gospel of Mark and Year C the Gospel of Luke. The Gospel of John is heard during

Easter and as needed during the rest of the year. The purpose of this is to ensure we receive a full and rich perspective from all of the Gospels over time.

The reflections in this book begin on January 1st, 2014 during the Christmas season. This was Year A in the lectionary using the Gospel of Matthew. It flows through the church's seasons and transitions to Year B on November 30, 2014 drawing from the Gospel of Mark during Advent and Christmas.

Catholic Mass in the Roman Rite includes Introductory Rites, Liturgy of the Word, Liturgy of the Eucharist, Communion Rite, prayer after communion and ends with the Concluding Rites.

The Liturgy of the Word on Sundays and Feast Days generally includes a reading from the Old Testament that is harmonized with the Gospel, a Psalm and an apostolic reading from the New Testament.

As you proceed, you will notice the name of each Sunday or feast day at the top of each *takeaway* page. The takeaway will be in the middle, and the scriptural passages used for that particular Mass will be listed at the bottom of each page. I've included a Psalm on the preceding page that is meant to harmonize with the takeaway.

The Catholic Church's liturgical structure of seasons and worship are its response to scripture and tradition handed down from the Apostles. Homilies by her priests seek to bring the word of God to life. The *takeaways* contained herein are a singular reflection on a particular day in response to hearing, praying, and reflecting on these words of scripture and the spoken proclamation of her priests. They hardly scratch the surface of the depth and breadth of God's message for us. What joy!

For E-Readers: The format of this book is optimized for print, but digital versions include hyperlinked scripture references to the relevant Bible passages on compatible devices for further reading and reflection.

"And your ears will hear a word behind you saying, this is the way, walk in it."

Isaiah 30:21

YEAR A

May God be gracious to us and bless us; may his face shine upon us.

Psalm 67:2

Mary, The Holy Mother of God

The appearance of the shepherds gave hope to His mother.

Mass Readings

Old Testament: Num 6:22-27
Psalm: PS 67:2a
New Testament: Gal 4:4-7
Gospel: Luke 2:16-21
January 1, 2014

May the kings of Tarshish and the islands bring tribute, the kings of Sheba and Seba offer gifts.

Psalm 72:10

Solemnity of the Epiphany of the Lord

The gifts of the Magi bolstered the faith of His foster father.

Is 60:1-6
Ps 72:1-2, 7-8, 10-11, 12-13
Eph 3:2-3a, 5-6
Mt 2:1-12
January 5, 2014

Give to the Lord the glory due His name. Bow down before the Lord's holy splendor!

Psalm 29:2

Feast of the Baptism of the Lord

He came for the humble and to give the arrogant pause.

Is 42:14, 6-7
Ps 29:1-2, 3-4, 3, 9-10
Acts 10:34-38
Mt 3:13-17
Jan 12, 2014

Blessed the man who sets his security in the Lord, who turns not to the arrogant or to those who stray after falsehood.

Psalm 40:5

Second Sunday in Ordinary Time

God was here, and He wants us to be joyous.

Is 49:3, 5-6
Ps 40:2, 4, 7-8, 8-9, 10
1 Cor 1:1-3
Jn 1:29-34
Jan 19, 2014

Third Sunday in Ordinary Time

Even if my father and mother forsake me, the Lord will take me in.

Psalm 27:10

Third Sunday in Ordinary Time

He wants us with him.

Is 8:23-9:3
Ps 27:1, 4, 13-14
1 Cor 1:10-13, 17
Mt 4:12-23
Jan 26, 2014

Who is the king of glory?

Psalm 24:10

Feast of the Presentation of the Lord

The Word of God was nurtured by a family.

Mal 3:1-4
Ps 24:7, 8, 9, 10
Heb 2:14-18
Lk 2:22-40
Feb 2, 2014

Fifth Sunday in Ordinary Time

Hallelujah! Blessed the man who fears the Lord, who greatly delights in his commands.

Psalm 112:1

Fifth Sunday in Ordinary Time

Try to make an impact because life is meant for living.

Is 58:7-10
Ps 112:4-5, 6-7, 8-9
1 Cor 2:1-5
Mt 5:13-16
Feb 9, 2014

It was good for me to be afflicted, in order to learn your statutes.

Psalm 119:71

Sixth Sunday in Ordinary Time

Try to be good rather than just seeming to be.

Sir 15:15-20
Ps 119:1-2, 4-5, 17-18, 33-34
1 Cor 2:6-10
Mt 5:17-37
Feb 16, 2014

He has not dealt with us as our sins merit, nor requited us as our wrongs deserve.

Psalm 103:10

Seventh Sunday in Ordinary Time

God is merciful beyond our understanding.

Lv 19:1-2, 17-18
Ps 103:1-2, 3-4, 8, 10, 12-13
1 Cor 3:16-23
Mt 5:38-48
Feb 23, 2014

My soul rests in God alone, from whom comes my salvation.

Psalm 62:2

Eighth Sunday in Ordinary Time

He suggests we keep things simple, less anxious that way.

Is 49:14-15
Ps 62:2-3, 6-7, 8-9
1 Cor 4:1-5
Mt 6:24-34
March 2, 2014

My sacrifice, O God, is a contrite spirit

Psalm 51:19

Ash Wednesday

Be charitable, pray and fast because they are good. This is reason enough.

Jl 2:12-18
Ps 51:3-4, 5-6ab, 12-13, 14 and 17
2 Cor 5:20-6:2
Mt 6:1-6, 16-18
March 5, 2014

Do not drive me from before your face, nor take from me your holy spirit.

Psalm 51:13

First Sunday of Lent

Be merciful O Lord, for we have sinned... All of us.

Gn 2:7-9; 3:1-7
Ps 51:3-4, 5-6, 12-13, 17
Rom 5:12-19
Mt 4:1-11
March 9, 2014

A king is not saved by a great army, nor a warrior delivered by great strength.

Psalm 33:16

Second Sunday of Lent

Do not be afraid. Listen to my son.

Gn 12:1-4a
Ps 33:4-5, 18-19, 20, 22
2 Tim 1:8b-10
Mt 17:1-9
March 16, 2014

Whose hand holds the depths of the earth; who owns the tops of the mountains?

Psalm 95:4

Third Sunday of Lent

God is involved because He cares about us. Every now and then he reminds us with a miracle.

Ex 17:3-7
Ps 95:1-2, 6-7, 8-9
Rom 5:1-2, 5-8
Jn 4:5-42
March 23, 2014

The Lord is my shepherd; there is nothing I lack.

Psalm 23:1

Fourth Sunday of Lent

Be open to the possibility that God is real and that His miracles make sense.

1 Sm 16:1b, 6-7, 10-13a
Ps 23:1-3a, 3b-4, 5, 6
Eph 5:8-14
Jn 9:1-41
March 30, 2014

Fifth Sunday of Lent

Out of the depths I call to you, Lord.

Psalm 130:1

Fifth Sunday of Lent

Everyone who lives and follows in Jesus' way will never die.

Ez 37:12-14
Ps 130:1-2, 3-4, 5-6, 7-8
Rom 8:8-11
Jn 11:1-45
April 6, 2014

My God, my God, why have you abandoned me?

Psalm 22:2

Palm Sunday of the Lord's Passion

God loves us like a father and then some.

Mt 21:1-11
Is 50:4-7
Ps 22:8-9, 17-18, 19-20, 23-24
Phil 2:6-11
Mt 26:14-27:66
April 13, 2014

Into your hands I commend my spirit

Psalm 31:6

Good Friday of the Lord's Passion

"With violence and torture let us put him to the test that we may have proof of his gentleness and try his patience. Let us condemn him to a shameful death; for according to his own words, God will take care of him."

Sirach 2:19-20

Is 52:13-53:12
Ps 31:2, 6, 12-13, 15-16, 17, 25
Heb 4:14-16; 5:7-9
Jn 18:1-19:42
April 18, 2014

The stone the builders rejected has become the cornerstone.

Psalm 118:22

Easter, Sunday – The Resurrection of the Lord

If God spoke to us directly, and told us what we needed to know, would we understand? Would we remember? Would we believe? But, if his Word died upon a cross and rose again...

Acts 10:34a, 37-43
Ps 118:1-2, 16-17, 22-23
Col 3:1-4 or 1 Cor 5:6b-8
Jn 20:1-9
April 20, 2014

The Lord is God and has enlightened us. Join in procession with leafy branches up to the horns of the altar.
Psalm 118:27

Second Sunday of Easter, Sunday of Divine Mercy

If you were God, knowing us as you do, how would you send word to us?

Acts 2:42-47
Ps 118:2-4, 13-15, 22-24
1 Pt 1:3-9
Jn 20:19-31
April 27, 2014

I keep the LORD always before me; with him at my right hand, I shall never be shaken.
Psalm 16:8

Third Sunday of Easter

Faith is a gift from God received through action during the journey of our lives.

Acts 2:14, 22-33
Ps 16:1-2, 5, 7-8, 9-10, 11
1 Pt 1:17-21
Lk 24:13-35
May 4, 2014

Indeed, goodness and mercy will pursue me all the days of my life; I will dwell in the house of the Lord for endless days.

Psalm 23:6

Fourth Sunday of Easter

God wants us to have abundant life.

Acts 2:14a, 36-41
Ps 23:1-2a, 3b-4, 5, 6
1 Pt 2:20b-25
Jn 10:1-10
May 11, 2014

By the Lord's word the heavens were made; by the breath of his mouth all their host.

Psalm 33:6

Fifth Sunday of Easter

You can believe because of the words or the works because whoever has seen Jesus has seen the Father.

Acts 6:1-7
Ps 33:1-2, 4-5, 18-19
1 Pt 2:4-9
Jn 14:1-12
May 18, 2014

But God did hear and listened to my voice in prayer.

Psalm 66:19

Sixth Sunday of Easter

I will not leave you orphans. I will come to you.

Acts 8:5-8, 14-17
Ps 66:1-3, 4-5, 6-7, 16, 20
1 Pt 3:15-18
Jn 14:15-21
May 25, 2014

One thing I ask of the Lord; this I seek: To dwell in the Lord's house all the days of my life, to gaze on the Lord's beauty, to visit his temple.

Psalm 27:4

Seventh Sunday of Easter

God is glorious!

Acts 1:12-14
Ps 27:1, 4, 7-8
1 Pt 4:13-16
Jn 17:1-11a
June 1, 2014

You make the winds your messengers;
flaming fire, your ministers.
Psalm 104:4

Pentecost

God places his spirit within us. The evidence is apparent in gifts like knowledge, courage, faith and humility.

Acts 2:1-11
Ps 104:1, 24, 29-30, 31, 34
1 Cor 12:3b-7, 12-13
Jn 20:19-23
June 8, 2014

The Lord says to my lord: “Sit at my right hand, while I make your enemies your footstool.”

Psalm 110:1

The Solemnity of the Most Holy Trinity

God wants us to know that there is eternal life for us.

Ex 34:4b-6, 8-9
Dn 3:52, 53, 54, 55, 56
2 Cor 13:11-13
Jn 3:16-18
June 15, 2014

The Solemnity of the Most Holy Body and Blood of Christ

Taste and see the Lord is good.

Psalm 34:9

The Solemnity of the Most Holy Body and Blood of Christ

God is real and present with us in His words, sacraments and the reality of our lives.

Dt 8:2-3, 14b-16a
Ps 147:12-13, 14-15, 19-20
1 Cor 10:16-17
Jn 6:51-58
June 22, 2014

The Solemnity of Saints Peter and Paul

I sought the Lord, and he answered me, delivered me from all my fears.

Psalm 34:5

The Solemnity of Saints Peter and Paul

A regular man named Peter believed that Jesus was the Son of God.

Acts 12:1-11
Ps 34:2-3, 4-5, 6-7, 8-9
2 Tm 4:6-8, 17-18
Mt 16:13-19
June 29, 2014

Fourteenth Sunday in Ordinary Time

The Lord supports all who are falling
and raises up all who are bowed down.
Psalm 145:14

Fourteenth Sunday in Ordinary Time

The more meek and humble we are, the closer to God we become.

Zec 9:9-10
Ps 145:1-2, 8-9, 10-11, 13-14
Rom 8:9, 11-13
Mt 11:25-30
July 6, 2014

Fifteenth Sunday in Ordinary Time

To you our vows must be fulfilled, you who hear our prayers.
Psalm 65:3

Fifteenth Sunday in Ordinary Time

When we understand God's Word we must do something with it.

Is 55:10-11
Ps 65:10, 11, 12-13, 14
Rom 8:18-23
Mt 13:1-23
July 13, 2014

Sixteenth Sunday in Ordinary Time

On the day of my distress, I call to you,
for you will answer me.

Psalm 86:7

Sixteenth Sunday in Ordinary Time

"The beginning of wisdom is fear of the Lord."

Sirach 1:14

Wis 12:13, 16-19
Ps 86:5-6, 9-10, 15-16
Rom 8:26-27
Mt 13:24-43
July 20, 2014

Seventeenth Sunday in Ordinary Time

From your judgments I do not turn,
for you have instructed me.
Psalm 119:102

Seventeenth Sunday in Ordinary Time

God gave us the ability to choose if we want to be with Him in Heaven.

1 Kgs 3:5, 7-12
Ps 119:57, 72, 76-77, 127-128, 129-130
Rom 8:28-30
Mt 13:44-52
July 27, 2014

Eighteenth Sunday in Ordinary Time

One generation praises your deeds to the next and proclaims your mighty works.

Psalm 145:4

Eighteenth Sunday in Ordinary Time

Jesus fed 5,000 men and even more women and children until they were full, and there were still leftovers.

Is 55:1-3
Ps 145:8-9, 15-16, 17-18
Rom 8:35, 37-39
Mt 14:13-21
Aug 3, 2014

Nineteenth Sunday in Ordinary Time

Love and truth will meet; justice and peace will kiss.

Psalm 85:11

Nineteenth Sunday in Ordinary Time

Jesus walked on water, and so they believed he was the Son of God.

1 Kgs 19:9a, 11-13a
Ps 85:9, 10, 11-12, 13-14
Rom 9:1-5
Mt 14:22-33
Aug 10, 2014

Assumption of the Blessed Virgin Mary

The queen stands at your right hand, arrayed in gold.

Psalm 45

Assumption of the Blessed Virgin Mary

Jesus was a good son and then some.

Rev 11:19; 12:1-6
Ps 45
Cor 15:20-27
Lk 1:39-56
Aug 10, 2014

Twentieth Sunday in Ordinary Time

So shall your way be known upon the earth, your victory among all the nations.

Psalm 67:3

Twentieth Sunday in Ordinary Time

A woman asked Jesus to heal her daughter and so he did.

Is 56:1, 6-7
Ps 67:2-3, 5, 6, 8
Rom 11:13-15, 29-32
Mt 15:21-28
Aug 17, 2014

Twenty-First Sunday in Ordinary Time

The Lord is on high, but cares for the lowly and knows the proud from afar.

Psalm 138:6

Twenty-First Sunday in Ordinary Time

Simon, son of Jonah, a poor fisherman believed that Jesus was the Christ, and this was enough to form the foundation of His church.

Is 22:19-23
Ps 138:1-2, 2-3, 6, 8
Rom 11:33-36
Mt 16:13-20
Aug 24, 2014

Twenty-Second Sunday in Ordinary Time

My soul clings fast to you; your right hand upholds me.

Psalm 63:9

Twenty-Second Sunday in Ordinary Time

To follow Jesus, we should try to be selfless despite our “crosses”.

Jer 20:7-9
Ps 63:2, 3-4, 5-6, 8-9
Rom 12:1-2
Mt 16:21-27
Aug 31, 2014

Twenty-Third Sunday in Ordinary Time

Oh, that today you would hear his voice and harden not your hearts.
Psalm 95:8

Twenty-Third Sunday in Ordinary Time

We have been given the power to forgive each other.

Ez 33:7-9
Ps 95:1-2, 6-7, 8-9
Rom 13:8-10
Mt 18:15-20
Sept 7, 2014

Feast of the Exaltation of the Holy Cross

I will open my mouth in a parable, unfold the puzzling events of the past.
Psalm 78:2

Feast of the Exaltation of the Holy Cross

We do not need to be ambivalent, aimless, or self-centered, nor afraid, or hungry for wealth and power, nor disempowered by blind fate or worried about death for God sent us Word, through Jesus, to let us know that there is a better way and that God is waiting for us in Heaven.

Nm 21:4b-9
Ps 78:1bc-2, 34-35, 36-37, 38
Phil 2:6-11
Jn 3:13-17
Sept 14, 2014

Twenty-Fifth Sunday in Ordinary Time

The Lord is gracious and merciful, slow to anger and abounding in mercy.
Psalm 145:8

Twenty-Fifth Sunday in Ordinary Time

Better for us that God is merciful in addition to being just.

Is 55:6-9
Ps 145:2-3, 8-9, 17-18
Phil 1:20c-24, 27a
Mt 20:1-16a
Sept 21, 2014

Twenty-Sixth Sunday in Ordinary Time

Make known to me your ways, Lord;
teach me your paths.
Psalm 25:4

Twenty-Sixth Sunday in Ordinary Time

Be careful to not let vanity or selfishness come between you and your pursuit of God's ways.

Ez 18:25-28
Ps 25:4-5, 8-9, 10, 14
Phil 2:1-11
Mt 21:28-32
Sept 28, 2014

Twenty-Seventh Sunday in Ordinary Time

Look down from heaven and see; visit this vine, the stock your right hand has planted, and the son whom you made strong for yourself.
Psalm 80:15

Twenty-Seventh Sunday in Ordinary Time

God holds us responsible to do our best with the gifts he has given to us.

Is 5:1-7
Ps 80:9, 12, 13-14, 15-16, 19-20
Phil 4:6-9
Mt 21:33-43
Oct 5, 2014

Twenty-Eighth Sunday in Ordinary Time

Indeed, goodness and mercy will pursue me all the days of my life
Psalm23:6

Twenty-Eighth Sunday in Ordinary Time

God is just.

Is 25:6-10a
Ps 23:1-3a, 3b-4, 5, 6
Phil 4:12-14, 19-20
Mt 22:1-14
Oct 12, 2014

Twenty-Ninth Sunday in Ordinary Time

Sing to the Lord a new song; sing to the Lord, all the earth.

Psalm 96:1

Twenty-Ninth Sunday in Ordinary Time

Be careful that your intelligence does not become a stumbling block to your faith in God.

Is 45:1, 4-6
Ps 96:1, 3, 4-5, 7-8, 9-10
1 Thes 1:1-5b
Mt 22:15-21
Oct 19, 2014

Thirtieth Sunday in Ordinary Time

I love you, Lord, my strength.

Psalm 18:2

Thirtieth Sunday in Ordinary Time

Love is the foundation for all of His rules, teachings and plans. So, if you make love the center of your whole life – what you think, say and do – then you are on His way!

Ex 22:20-26
Ps 18:2-3, 3-4, 47, 51
1 Thes 1:5c-10
Mt 22:34-40
Oct 26, 2014

The Commemoration of All the Faithful Departed (All Souls)

Even though I walk through the valley of the shadow of death, I will fear no evil, for you are with me

Psalm 23:4

The Commemoration of All the Faithful Departed (All Souls)

We beg to differ! Death is not the end of our lives.

Is 25:6-9
Ps 23:1-3a, 3b-4, 5, 6
Thes 4:13-18 or Rom 6:3-9
Mat 5:1-12
Nov 2, 2014

The Feast of the Dedication of the Lateran Basilica in Rome

Be still and know that I am God!
Psalm 46:11

The Feast of the Dedication of the Lateran Basilica in Rome

Jesus created a church with a purpose.

Ez 47:1-2, 8-9, 12
Ps 46:2-3, 5-6, 8-9
1 Cor 3:9c-11, 16-17
Jn 2:13-22
Nov 9, 2014

Thirty-third Sunday in Ordinary Time

Blessed are all who fear the Lord, and who walk in his ways.

Psalm 128:1

Thirty-third Sunday in Ordinary Time

Please use your talent to its full potential.

Prv 31:10-13, 19-20, 30-31
Ps 128:1-2, 3, 4-5
1 Thes 5:1-6
Mt 25:14-30
Nov 16, 2014

The Solemnity of Our Lord Jesus Christ, King of the Universe

He restores my soul. He guides me along right paths for the sake of his name.

Psalm 23:3

The Solemnity of Our Lord Jesus Christ, King of the Universe

Take care of each other, especially those who need it the most.

Ez 34:11-12, 15-17
Ps 23:1-2, 2-3, 5-6
1 Cor 15:20-26, 28
Mt 25:31-46
Nov 23, 2014

YEAR B

Lord God of hosts, restore us; light up your face and we shall be saved.
Psalm 80:20

First Sunday of Advent

Stive to be virtuous (every day).

Is 63:16b-17, 19b; 64:2-7
Ps 80:2-3, 15-16, 18-19
1 Cor 1:3-9
Mk 13:33-37
Nov 30, 2014

Show us, Lord, your mercy; grant us your salvation.
Psalm 85:8

Second Sunday of Advent

Jesus was not a scientist. Nor was he an economist, soldier, politician or entertainer. Instead of all these he was a savior.

Is 40:1-5, 9-11
Ps 85:9-10, 11-12, 13-14
2 Pt 3:8-14
Mk 1:1-8
Dec 7, 2014

The Feast of the Immaculate Conception of the Blessed Virgin Mary

All the ends of the earth have seen the victory of our God.

Psalm 98:3

The Feast of the Immaculate Conception of the Blessed Virgin Mary

Angels are real! Demons, too. Thank God for Mary!

Gen 3:9-15, 20
Psalm 98
Eph 1:3-6, 11-12
Lk 1:26-38
Dec 14, 2014

My soul proclaims the greatness of the Lord; my spirit rejoices in God my savior.

Luke 1:46

Third Sunday of Advent

Look forward! The best is yet to come.

Is 61:1-2a, 10-11
Lk 1:46-48, 49-50, 53-54
1 Thes 5:16-24
Jn 1:6-8, 19-28
Dec 14, 2014

Fourth Sunday of Advent

My mercy is established forever; my faithfulness will stand as long as the heavens.

Psalm 89:3

Fourth Sunday of Advent

"Hail Mary, full of grace! The Lord is with you."

2 Sm 7:1-5, 8b-12, 14a, 16
Ps 89:2-3, 4-5, 27-29
Rom 16:25-27
Lk 1:26-38
Dec 21, 2014

Shout with joy to the Lord, all the earth; break into song; sing praise.
Psalm 98:4

The Nativity of the Lord (Christmas)

"And the Word became flesh and made His dwelling among us."

Is 52:7-10
Ps 98:1, 2-3, 3-4, 5-6
Heb 1:1-6
Jn 1:1-18
Dec 25, 2014

Blessed are all who fear the Lord, and who walk in his ways.
Psalm 128:1

The Holy Family of Jesus, Mary and Joseph

For what purpose did the "Word of God" come to us in the form of a man if it was not to teach us His Way.

Sir 3:2-6, 12-14 or Gn 15:1-6; 21:1-3
Ps 128:1-2, 3, 4-5 or Ps 105:1-2, 3-4, 5-6, 8-9
Col 3:12-21 or Heb 11:8, 11-12, 17-19
Lk 2:22-40
Dec 28, 2014

A PRAYER ARISING

TEACH ME YOUR WAY

Dear Jesus, please teach me Your Way.
Help me to live in the present when I am scared.
Remind me to be humble always and everywhere.
Help me to simplify when I am worried.
Remind me of Your presence when I am sad.
Let me hear Your Word when I am ambivalent.
Feed me Your Eucharist when my faith falters.
Have mercy on me when I feel proud.
Let me appreciate Your glory when I am happy.
Help me to be present, loving, and wise
for all who need me.

And, in everything I do, please give me strength to remain on Your way.

Amen.

ABOUT THE AUTHOR

William E. Bullis brings over four decades of work experience spanning the computer and medical device industries, working in the fields of I.T., research and development, and manufacturing. A lifelong Catholic, Bill lives near Pittsburgh, Pennsylvania, with his wife of thirty-nine years, Leslie. Together, they raised three children.

Teach Me Your Way is his second book - written before but published after *Am I Really Catholic? The Presidents Daughter Is Surprised by Her Faith*.

Made in the USA
Las Vegas, NV
15 November 2025

4ace95b4-8b24-4a7c-aaa3-9879b484d13cR01